Fluttering Hands

Stephen W.

Stephen Wilson

To Petronel,
With good wishes,
Feb 2010

GREENWICH EXCHANGE
LONDON

Greenwich Exchange, London

Fluttering Hands

© Stephen Wilson 2008

First published in Great Britain in 2008
All rights reserved

Printed and bound by Q3 Digital/Litho, Loughborough
Tel: 01509 213456
Typesetting and layout by Albion Associates, London
Tel: 020 8852 4646
Cover design by December Publications, Belfast
Tel: 028 90286559

Cover image shows a DETAIL from Marc Chagall's painting *Song of Songs* series No.III, (1960) Marc Chagall Museum, Nice, France.
© ADAGP, Paris and DACS, London 2008
Photograph © Visions of America, LLC/Alamy

Greenwich Exchange Website: www.greenex.co.uk

Cataloguing in Publication Data is available from the British Library.

ISBN-13: 978-1-906075-19-4
ISBN-10: 1-906075-19-0

To Eva, Rosie and Mia for the future

ACKNOWLEDGEMENTS

Some of these poems (or earlier versions) appeared in *Brand*, *The Interpreter's House*, *The Jewish Quarterly*, *The Liberal*, *The London Review of Books*, *Magma*, *The New Welsh Review*, *Oxford Magazine*, *Poetry Durham*, *The Reader*, *The Rialto*, *Stand*, *The Wolf* and in the *The Barnet Poetry Anthology* 2006, *Solitaire*, (Templar Poetry, 2007) and *Wild* (Wyvern Works, 2007). 'Can I Take Your Coat', 'Names' and 'Footprints' won prizes in *Poetry News*. 'Needlework' won a prize in The Blackwell Publishing/The Reader Poetry Competition, 2006. 'Canzone', 'Dazzlement', 'Welsh-English Dictionary' and 'Conservation Studio: Hermitage', were digitalised for the Poetry Library, Southbank Centre. 'Conservation Studio: Hermitage' was also recorded.

I am especially grateful to Kate Wilson and Matthew Francis for their encouragement and editorial comments.

Contents

I

II

III

I

Shepherd's Delight

We hadn't actually asked for advice
but something must have made him
recommend duck eggs.

Perhaps we were having a row
or had been knackered by the hike
and looked needy?

More likely he was bored, having spoken
to no one but a straggle of girls
doing their Duke of Edinburgh Award

on Sugarloaf Mountain; maybe we seemed
low in erotic energy, off-heat
like parents whose kids don't sleep

or rams ~~in wintertime~~ *unsound*. Anyway,
the answer was duck eggs.
Five months after tupping, he camped

in a shelter crammed with buckets,
ropes and snares, vaseline, iodine,
syringes, needles, teated beer bottles

under a blue pasture where the clouds
scarcely moved – pregnant ewes
enjoying the sun, just waiting

for the weather to settle –
it wouldn't be long. Flicking
a tail of ash off a fag, he suggested

we pack the raw eggs in a paste
of burnt pine needles, tea, charcoal
and salt, for a hundred days

till their shells turned amber and whites
had a stony 'thousand-year' appearance –
nothing like a short diet-course.

Llywellyn's wife said lambing
was her annual holiday.
He called it his annual divorce.

Welsh-English Dictionary

Table of mutations

When preceded by a d,
the m
mutates into an f,
which is pronounced v.

When preceded by a shop,
the leaving
mutates into a farewell,
which is pronounced ta-da.

When preceded by a shearer,
the sheep
mutates into a shiver,
which is pronounced shorn.

When preceded by a mew,
the red kite's fork
mutates into a fan,
which is pronounced buzzard.

When preceded by a sou'westerly,
the earth
mutates into the Irish sea,
which is pronounced inundation.

When preceded by a pigeon-fancier,
the peregrine falcon
mutates into carrion,
which is pronounced dead.

When preceded by a coal-face,
the man
mutates into a case,
which is pronounced pneumoconiosis.

When preceded by winter,
the black mountain
mutates into a white rhino,
which is pronounced wonderful.

Hillfarm

Beads of dung dropped under blackthorn
as from a broken thread …
we've footed this path before,
seen dogs chase a ewe into Wastwater,
its cold weakening,
collie mouthing head;
a sheep enmeshed, galvanised,
eyeless before its time.

But now upside-down,
stuck two hooves
in the cloven wire
like a strung-up lynch
or prisoner reached
the perimeter, shot imperfectly.
Just hear the laboured breath,
heart work and I can't

release the tension −
it'll hang till lung-ed out,
spirit blown,
skull beaked to ivory,
a towel stiffened by winter
as if weather should want
to dry hands on a track
in the smudge of a haze.

Flightpath

A465, Heads of the Valleys Road

Despite the talent for miniaturisation –
a tiny handlebar moustache bristling with sonar,

and notwithstanding the art of hanging upside down,
bivouacked in its own wings for long periods,

on the roofs of caves, attics and boiler rooms,
to say nothing of the Lesser Horseshoe's

enviable ability to zoom low at night,
homing in on gnats and crane flies;

its single-minded trajectory,
elsewhere a virtue, is fatal

when it comes to crossing roads.
Blind to human traffic, its failed parachute

just keeps dropping to the lowest linear feature.
Who'd ever heard of bats needing bridges,

suspended high over the carriageway like safety nets
in a flying circus, or some theatre of the absurd?

A Year in the Beacons

White streaks arc the current's bubble-burst,
the dippers' own springing energy,
faster than foam, than my eye can see,
water-birds made from flying water,
cascade the Mellte's borborygmi,
melt in its simmer, hidden
on boulders of millstone-grit.

Between low cloud and alto-stratus
an engine rasps the summer silence –
obscure as the uplift of a lark,
insistent as an unwanted guest.
Then the wind forces a crescendo,
like an unseen hand putting
a giant conch to both ears.

Bracken, the autumn's flaming harvest –
whole hillsides bloom in the heat, send up
red and yellow flowers, black nimbi,
cathedral domes rising in the sky,
ornate thuribles swinging ash-waft.
Next year's fronds will sprout again,
unclipping the fire-bird's wings.

Winter bites off more than it can chew,
picks the tree-bones clean, spatters the orts
on a wizened salad of has-beens.
Fallen regiments are underfoot,
their trampled limbs – oak, ash, beech and thorn.
At the grounding of the sun,
no one will remember them.

Wordsworth Inventories
the Contents of a Welsh Cloud

Tarmac, the steady drip of down-pipes,
PVC casements, slim-line storage heaters,
Selwyn at the bar, recalling the time
his pelvis was crushed by a JCB
he was dieseling up for the colliery,
and how his private parts swelled
to the size of water-melons.
Ice-cream vans layby-ed –

waiting for the mist to clear.
Sheep, coughing like retired miners
or lying like moth-eaten rags
on the locker-room floor.
Shreds of blue and white plastic,
(optimistically) hung out to dry.
Hedgerows, dated by species of can and crisp,
it's about as lonely as the last eisteddfod.

Colour-Blind Romance

after Lorca's Romance Sonámbulo

How can I love what I cannot see?
Green, green, I love you green.
Sun on a woodland canopy,
how can I see what can't be seen?

Green bird on an olive-branch,
how can I love what I cannot see?
Green waves on the meadow grass,
how can I say what it is to me?

Green, green, I love you green.
Green light in a purple sky,
how can I love what I cannot see?
Fishing barque in the aquamarine,

scarlet buds on the rowan tree,
how can I see what can't be seen?
Chestnut horse in a snort of steam,
how can I love what I've never seen?

Juvenile Magnolia

All year long I've been waiting
on the promise of a light green
cocoon whose size increased in
almost imperceptible increments
its tepals unable to free themselves
yet always on the point of budburst
as if something inside couldn't
quite prise them open, wasn't
strong enough to force their hand
or didn't know its own best interest
until now, early September
when after daybreak –
the white arch of a bird's wings
nesting alone on a terminal bract
mute, unmarked, belonging
I presume to Her Majesty the Queen
– Seigneur of the Swans.

The Reincarnation of Leaves

Bija niyama lights
the blue touch-paper.
Pirouettes of sky-divers

dancing for joy or death –
ah! how they turn and twist,
sparkle, fall and rise again

as yellowhammers, redstarts,
firecrests and chiffchaffs,
winged on the prayer of passing cars.

Cold Then Hot

Today it's dropped to minus five,
the world's displayed through screens –
iced window-sashes, glazed casements.
Outside the air's frosted the trees into
starched bridesmaids at a wedding-shoot.

But we're lounging like Caesars watching
the amphitheatre in the woodburner,
listening to the murmur of the crowd,
the sudden insuck of expectation
as the tigers start their evening prowl.

Pennipotenti

i Buteo Buteo

The lime kiln's an abandoned roost,
single hawthorn, bent spine
fired by the wind, fingerpost
on the hill's crest – they're up there
watching a fallen cow
trapped in a shake-hole –
Joseph calling his brothers
from beneath the ground,
dreams a pair of winged cats
mewing in the sky
and for a moment thinks
Why not me – high over Sarn Helen
searching the clints,
lazy on warm air,
spotting a scarab out of a grike.

ii Columba Livia

Ooh, ah, always in a flap, a fluster,
they're yes-men who dress

up their lack of character
with bluster, pomp and strut,

stuff-shirts, shits, grey-men,
city-slickers living on the ledge,

the land's fat, fatter by the day
on business lunches and claiming

all the time to eat like birds till
they turn to intractable cases,

yesterday's men in guanoed squares
now become open air clinics

for bulimic squabs, or fetch up
on a health farm where someone

swaps their suits for bulging leotards
and recommends more exercise –

Indian dancing – a personal trainer,
a siskin holding tail-feathers out straight

like a yellow Lycra-ed trapeze artist
or gymnast working the asymmetric bars.

iii Larus Argentatus

An unpalatable truth,
the herring gull's success
derives from an ability
to eat almost anything,
even young of its own kind.
Have you seen silver-back
always looking over his shoulder?
Watch him find a rotting sandwich,
a dead fish, a piece of rope,
a newborn seal pup's placenta,
approach like a bomb disposal expert –
one snip of the yellow wire cutters
and he's up with the wind.

iv Cygnus Olor

It's the bad swan season. Last week a pen
with a broken leg, how did that happen?
And now a swaddle of grey feathers
velcroed into the back of your ute,
dead I thought at first, till its head came
swanning over, one enquiring eye
giving me the once over, staring from
out its strait-jacket, only the neck,
tangled in nylon, moving as if charmed
from a bag, but there was no music,
just a whimper as you opened the dark beak,
nostrils indignant, and took the hook-barb
from its tongue with a pair of bull-nosed pliers,
mute anger held taut under the folded wings.

v Pica Pica

A pair of magpies leaves the fence,
like nuns hurrying to mass on a windy day.
But nuns don't chack like broken gearboxes
or pick through bin-bags like junkies trying
to steal your identity. On the other hand
magpies have been known to warble,
like nuns singing their hymns.
I've heard it said, in parts of the antipodes,
nuns are like Hitchcock's birds,
they can swoop out of a clear sky
and trephine a man's scalp in no time.
The farmer who told me this was bald
and stood at greater risk, he could be wrong.
If nuns are up there at all, they must be
less like hags flying on broomsticks
and more like doves in an early Chagall.

vi Phasianus Colchicus

It was too late to brake, impossible to swerve –
what bird-brained philosophy made it plod on
oblivious, as if it had its mind on higher things
and wasn't to be disturbed? Bottle-green head,
cheeks wattled red, neck stretched forward
like it was pulling against a leash,
turning an indifferent eye, deaf ear to my horn.
It was one of those times when the future
is suddenly certain, or there is no future,
when there's nothing to do but hold course –
and I thought of you on a strange road
leaning into a bend, that day a pheasant
from nowhere flew across your front wheel;
and felt like some avenging angel.

vii Brace

Lagopus Scoticus

When Prince Albert planned
the Great Exhibition of 1851
as a token of British industrial
might, he assembled a committee
to oversee the erection
of a vast pavilion in Hyde Park,
which included Sir Joseph Paxton
and Isambard Kingdom Brunel.
Fashioned from cast-iron and glass,
the structure stood on a site
measuring nearly a million square feet,
and was put up in nine months.

Inside *The Crystal Palace*,
frock-coats and crinolines,
silver-topped canes, small children,
jostled past working machines.
Spoked flywheels ratcheted up
the cylinder-shafts, spools
and sprockets. McNicholl's
travelling crane was there,
James Nasmyth's steam hammer,
Harrison's power loom and
the grand *Lord of the Isles*, pride
of the Great Western Railway.

Somewhere among the printing
presses, reaping apparatus
and steel-making displays,
they found room for a grouse
perched on a mahogany block,
beneath which embossed in brass,
a caption edged like a Christmas
card in twining holly:
THIS BIRD HAS BEEN
MOUNTED AND STUFFED BY
IVOR POAKE (Taxidermists) LTD
68A, THE STRAND, LONDON.

Tetrao Tetrix (Celticus)

One imagines he died
or was taken suddenly
from the cottage,
leaving everything
just as it was, tied
to the 2nd Viscount Tredegar
(soon too to be extinct),
Evan Frederick Morgan's
Estate, nothing but rough
grass, bracken and reeds,
the barren moors tufting
endless toward Cefn Cadlan,

Cadair Fawr. And within
the lichened stones a letter
on the table, enquiring as to
the prospects for shooting
blackcock and greyhen
that year – end June, 1946,
reply required a.s.a.p.
On the back, Dafyd Jones
experimenting with the crook
of his name and address,
Hepste-Fechan in copper plate.

viii Skein

Branta Canadensis

There go my boys –
a chevron of honkers,
hooligans, attention-seekers,
elegant as a line
of three-quarters,
fanning out to the wing.

Swarm

Forget the hive, the old queen's gone
followed by fifty-thousand paparazzi
and you, in your scarlet van,
with the drone emblazoned
where I'd expect 'Royal Mail' to be,
chasing a shadow in the sky,
some kind of u.f.o.
heading god-knows-where.
But there, on a distant post
is it a bird or hiker's glove
waiting to be found? Maybe no more
than a dollop of creosote
thickly applied, yet it's alive –

Take an oil-can with bellows attached,
perhaps a tin klaxon for makeshift music.
Hand cupped over its mouth,
you drop a match in a clod of rags
and puff clouds from the spout,
cover them in confusion.
Then, like a demon-barber making a blow-wave
or member of some noxious hooded clan,
you brush the hum into a cardboard box.
What's amazing is the way they all surrender,
like fans converging on a football ground
or shoppers at a New Year's Sale,
as if that empty trap was packed
with lavender and broom. It means she's got.
There's not a lick of nectar to be had,
but they'd buzz anywhere for a whiff of her scent.

Snow

is born without a tongue
schooled by our boots
learns to croak
like frogs in amplexus

in mid-life
comes by a siege mentality
grows prudish
utters nothing but shush

turns morose when old
hangs its sheepskin
on the hedgerows
and leaves us weeping

II

Geest Star

Three days out of strike-bound Liverpool,
we began throwing the bananas overboard.
Hauling up the heavy cargo of cold green fruit
from the hold, lobbing the stems from man to man –

the ocean took it all; fuel-efficient
now, the Star rolled in the swell.
Cups, plates, bowls and eating-irons slid
on dampened table-cloths, as the Officer's
meatballs went flying in their Mess

and the passengers (there were only three)
immured in their cabins, watched the sea rise
and fall in the misty eye of a ship's porthole.
One was a Czech émigrée-nun going to a leprosarium
in Dominica. When the warm air mellowed,

the Company wore white. And at the Tropic
of Cancer, the deck was strewn with winged fish –
hapless birdmen, blown over the edge
of their world. We were heading for
the Antilles. All the while in mind –

land, bread-fruit, and the chant of that first
son-of-a-slave in Bridgetown:
I like it. De-man-wavin.

Meltemi

The boats are old men
who never stop moaning.
I am an old man.
The boats are autistic children
who never stop rocking.
I am an autistic child.
The boats are tied in
with stern-lines.
The children are tongue-tied.
The old men creak with tiredness.
Sometimes we all
bang spoons on the table,
tinkle high pitched bells,
tread on each other's toes.
I am making a catalogue of groans.
I will ask the masts to listen.
I will take away their crosstrees.
I will apply wire-cutters to their stays.
I will remove their antennae,
their wind instruments, their cruising lights.
Tomorrow I will bring them down.

The Language of Small Fishing Boats

At sundown
a floating four-poster,
candy-striped awning
moving slowly over the water,
drowning the sea's gossip
with the pluck pluck pluck
of its engine.

Another one astern
tutting repeatedly
as it hands out nets
like food-aid for starving fish.
After dark the Touretter
comes out rehearsing
a soliloquy of fucks.

Gloucester, Mass.

Jet-saved, America wowed us.
Air-conditioned and cruise-controlled
we hired an Olds and travelled
in formation at fifty on the turnpike.

The road outside was hot-like-hell
and dusty, we headed for the ocean
longing to swim…

and found a latter-day Canute
swinging his baton. Like
it wasn't real when he blew
the whistle on us, saying –
Sorry lady, the sea's closed.

Cardigan Bay

In my room on the promenade,
Queensbridge Hotel,
I raise high the attic sash,
let the brushes work my eardrums –

all night long the sea's maracas,
the pebble-plash and drag,
faint scent of bladderwrack,
cool North Beach jazz,

playing to an empty pavilion,
not even a gull on the balustrade,
only the clap clap clap of the waves,
indifferent as sleepwalkers,

as Johnny Cobb on percussion
or Miles Davis turning his back.

The Sea

                       's unrolling her hair in the mirror,
brushing it out; returning unwanted gifts
like Lady Muck: a length of hawser,
thick as Ahab's thigh, dumped near Oxwich cliff;
a plastic bottle collection, a set of storage utensils –
pallets, crates and kegs – a drum kit
for a steel band, tea chests, two spare wheels,
beach-balls, frisbees, a metal-detecting-outfit;
sculptured tree limbs, flayed white; a nest of nylon string,
wicker pots, linen tads, a lilo and bodyboard;
a donkey-tailed warp, deckchair and swimwear; bunting,
an amputee doll, windbreak and snorkel;
cheapjack pearls, splintered planks and sandal-soles.
Ah, but she keeps her beaten gold!

Byng

Sir, I have the pleasure to desire
that you will acquaint their Lordships
that having sailed from Gibraltar,

eleven days heeled into the wind,
we got off Mahon; His Majesty's colours
resplendent on Fort St Philip –

round-shot skidding up the bastion walls.
Sixteen thousand Frenchmen
to a hundred of my fusiliers, unable to land,

untrained in combat at sea.
I made plans to reconnoitre the harbour,
dispatched *Phoenix*, *Chesterfield* and *Dolphin*,

with a letter ashore. The enemy's fleet,
appearing to the south-east, just as the wind
came strong off the land, obliged me

to call ships in before having found
the disposition of their ordnance.
Twelve ships of the line, and three frigates;

against ten vessels in disrepair. As night fell,
I tacked to keep the weather-gage. By daylight
there were none to be seen save at our rear,

two tartars with the French private signal,
which we chased. *Defiance* took two captains,
two lieutenants and one hundred and two private soldiers.

From the mast-head we sighted the enemy
forming a line to leeward (having failed to weather me);
Phoenix offered herself as a fire-ship.

At two, I made the signal to engage, ordering every ship
to close down on the one that fell to their lot.
Unfortunately, *Intrepid*'s foretopmast was shot away

causing it to foul her sail, which backed
so that the ship was not under command;
her fore-tack and braces being cut,

she drove onto the next ship
causing that and the ships ahead of me
to throw all back, lest they too fall on each other.

Once having destroyed our rigging,
I found the enemy edged away constantly,
would not permit our closing with them –

their ships were clean, bearing three feet to one of ours.
We refitted through the night. At dawn I sent cruisers
to bring me the state and condition of the squadron:

Captain, Intrepid and *Defiance* were much damaged in their
masts.
Many were sick, killed and wounded, and nowhere to put
a third of their number if I made a hospital of the forty-gun.

Minorca was at risk but so was the rock.
I summoned a council of war,
desiring the opinion of General Stuart, Lord Effingham,

Lord Robert Bertie and Colonel Cornwallis.
Since we could neither succour nor relieve the former,
logic dictated we protect the latter.

Our loss was heavy, yet we may justly claim victory,
having caused the enemy to withdraw. With reinforcement,
I will not lose a moment of time in seeking him.

Yet I have been troubled by a waking dream:
my effigy, white waistcoat richly edged in gold,
burnt on pyres up and down the land. Me blindfold,

kneeling on the quarterdeck, handkerchief in hand,
before a company of marines, while someone reads
the Articles of War: Admiral the Honourable John Byng –

failing to do his utmost to relieve St Philip's Castle
in the Island of Minorca; failing to do his utmost
to take, seize and destroy the ships of the French King.

III

Conservation Studio: Hermitage

I'm wearing my fur hat like a patriarch's
klobuk, as if it conferred the privilege
of entering the museum by a side door.

Igor Borisovich lets us in. He's Leo Tolstoy,
he's a dancing bear, Russian as an iconostasis
from Novgorod or the Church on Spilled Blood.

We've climbed to an attic overlooking the Neva
and you ask if your handbag will be safe
on the floor. He says, We leave Leonardos there.

Who'd ever know it's a Madonna on his easel?
She's like a tinted window in a stretch-limo
or slice of toast covered in Marmite.

Peeled off her bed of oak during the dark ages
and laid on canvas like a sliver of skin
grafted to a burn or logo on a t-shirt.

It was the sturgeon's air-bladders
that stuck her down, soaked in water,
blended with honey and squeezed to a pulp,

then warmed, like a delicacy taken
at the Mariinskiy between acts.
Note the properties of whitefish glue, he says,

that make it a perfect icon for our State – plastic
like perestroika, yet strong as the Kremlin wall
and good at penetrating into small crevices.

Yucca Moth

Cross-dressed – in a golden helmet,
a pollen-ball three times the size
   of her own head –
conquistador, she comes in the night,
fires eggs into the flower's ovary.
Strong wind off the Gulf of Campeche,
women behind men

freighting firewood tied in henequen.
Look, the armadillos
   are balling up
and a plucked hen's running about
as if the Zapatistas were on their way.
Where are the yucca's bayonets?
The sapodilla weeps white

aching like a wet-nurse.
Remember the cold hills
   of the Chiapas
my love, how we plundered weaves
off the floor for a wrap. Picture Francisco
Hernandez de Cordoba and his horse –
that naked chicken, that shivering moth.

After *The Triumph of Death*

by Brueghel the Elder

A green bone-man scythes the traffic
for fifteen seconds, busks grotesque
birdsong walking on the spot.
Two long black Mercedes halt

on the stop line. I look right instead of left,
falter like a pensionista. Midway across,
the cars begin a low-pitched dirge –
this much, at least, I can understand:

you will quit the train at Atocha Renfe
and be in the Plaza de Murillo
at one o'clock outside the Prado;
that nothing is certain now in Madrid

and that if you're not there
within half an hour, I shouldn't wait.

Camille c1890

Study the etching for five minutes, then write down
all the objects you can see hidden in Pissarro's face.
Bear in mind he was born in St Thomas of Jewish stock,
would have been familiar with the breadfruit tree
and later fell in love with a Parisian kitchen maid.
Do not forget that berets, although soft, can conceal
a deep hatred for bourgeois society; that half-moons
worn just below the bridge of the nose, can reflect light
in such a way as to give the impression of surprise.
Remember that no pigment is used in his whiskers
yet they are incandescent, whiter than titanium-white.
Access to the area behind the beard can be gained
by entering the artist's portrait through the open eyes.
Can you make out Madame Julie Pissarro, worried
by the lack of money as she does her needlework?
Undo a stash of letters from his son Lucien and find
a sketch of Esther Bensusan, standing in front
of her father's warehouse, full of ostrich feathers.
See if you can spot four naked peasant girls,
bathing in a stream by a thicket, or clothed women
driving pea-stakes into the ground. Look out for a field
of ripe wheat, and try to understand how there could be
   'nothing more cold than the full summer sun'.

Can I Take Your Coat

Let's work back through it all,
starting with the outer layers –
first, today's residue, dark-eyes,

bad-feels, brushed aside only
to reveal a tissue of thorns,
too much history that could be

poisonous and needs to be removed.
What's left, an indifferent varnish,
cracked like parched earth or dry lips,

dissolves slowly in methylated spirit
dabbed on with a cotton-wool bud.
Next, there's a viscous pigment,

purple bound in egg, a clinginess
that spreads all over you and must
be pared away with a scalpel blade.

And then, at last, the original picture,
dove-white streaks on cobalt blue,
love's wind in the sea's feathers.

Cocksure

That time I peed under a lamppost
as the bulb came on,
was worth the apple in my mother's eye,
spelt more wonders
than a fountain jet played against a wall
or golden rapier
crossed in a swordfight. At sunset,
a young dog
taken by surprise; how the street
glowed yellow
splashed in the xanthic power of my spring.
I was Leerie,
Magic Lamplighter, not the child
waiting on his nod.

Relics

apart from the long shovel
meant for sprinkling dry sand
onto burning magnesium
and the galvanised iron tub
in which I supposed the flames
were dunked where on hot days
I took respite from the sun
submerging as much of my body
as I could like a boiled chicken
in a pan

there was the gas-mask
the tin helmet the stirrup pump
and uncle Harold's Sam Browne
with its empty leather holster
fastened with a brass stud
that I wore slung around my hips
like Wyatt Earp leaving a saloon
or Gary Cooper in High Noon

but without the gun my uncle
must have used to kill Germans
in the battle of Monte Casino
which was stashed away
at the top of the broom-cupboard
shrouded in oily rags and later
decommissioned by my father
who dropped it in the Thames
when no one was looking

Uncle Simon's Eighty-Fifth

Milk, you insist, can be emptied
from a glass jug into a paper cone,
that (staying miraculously dry)
can be screwed up and tossed away.
The secret is a hidden case
into which the poured milk flows.
I recall the many occasions
on which you removed your thumb
and stuck it back, triumphantly
produced aces from a shuffled pack
or spirited a handkerchief into thin air.
And now the magic again –
My lips know your stubble
as a kiss on the Land of Israel,
the pleasure of a forgotten home.
Out of our embrace, warm
like a dove conjured from a fist,
your brother, my father – alive.

Chimaera

Believe me little brother, the skeleton
in the ghost train was a flash of neon,
the ghoulish touch was a peacock feather;
the waltzers never danced; most of the coconuts
were stuck down.

Somebody had tampered with the rifle sights
and the number under your floating duck
wouldn't come up with a bear that size.
We could've shot, fished and shied
all day, still slunk home without a prize.

Waiting to enter the rat-woman's tent
I could smell a creature half human,
half rodent, female torso and hairless tail –
we should've had our shilling back
from that caged slut in a sequinned leotard,
holding court with a tribe of rats.

Say it was a lesson in tat, in disenchanted dreams,
searching for magic in the candyfloss machine.

From the Anatomy Room

Riding the Circle line in rush-hour
I was the body under suspicion,
the one that wasn't using *Amplex*
didn't wash with *Lifebuoy.*
Odd the way those seats beside me
stayed unfilled till Baker Street.
Straps hung like unpicked fruit,
commuters turned their backs –
they say a fox can't smell its lair,
but this was different; a foetid blend
of antiseptic sickly-sweet,
a lab-coat you couldn't take off,
a stigma reeking from the skin.

Where I'd been the shelves were stacked
with specimens in jars of formalin,
a devil's pantry on display. The place
was polished like a well-kept ward
with patients down each side
in tidy rows – they never called
a nurse, or moved their toes.

Restoration

You must have escaped in a hurry
dropping so many little intimacies
from our lives – thermal-vests, long-johns,
a lace camisole, a black bow-tie,
a packet of Tampax on the floor beside the bed,
my old tennis-shoes
(were your backs done in too?).

I picture your arrival, through the rockery,
sinking your feet into heather,
shrugging off rhododendron branches,
strands of honeysuckle; prizing
open the sash with an iron bar,
your bodies folded like contortionists
among slivers of glass and wood.

Surgeons in a slapstick
operation, you don rubber gloves
still wet with Fairy foam,
and choose the right knife
for the job. You have turned
our house into a fading Caravaggio,

which the men from the Incident Room
lovingly restore. When the silvery powder
is brushed away, we can see
exactly what you fingered;
a textured print of small circles,
like suckers on an octopus tentacle,
softly formicate under our skin.

Stones

I wondered what had got you down –
the move, the house (in more than usual
disarray) coated in a glutinous film
of dried up food and dust; arguments
over every decision when we climbed
Clifford's Tower, where the Jews
of York had torched themselves.
A tour of the cemetery didn't
immediately strike me as desirable;
to stand in that gaping iron gateway
and rub hands as if to raise a spark,
like patients waiting for some windswept
necro-therapy. We wanted an answer
to the erosion, but nothing seemed enough.
A starfish tentacle clinging to the letters
of an epitaph, a piece of shell washed
to the surface of a limestone sea,
equatorial sand-dunes, sea-urchins
and brachiopods. Pre-historic mare's tails
still growing in the grass, a dinosaur's footprint?

Bad Neighbours

You guarded that stretch of tarmac like a wild swan –
parking on your side evoked the beating wings,
the urgent hiss, the stranger response. No matter
we lived in spitting distance, you plastered warnings

on the windscreen so fast we called you Mrs Nasty,
laughed you off and waited for your nemesis to come.
And Mr Nasty never missed a trick, watched the street
like a trainee traffic warden, a special PC

flush with authority; until we saw him on your arm,
wearing dark glasses and tapping a white stick.
We could've left our car on double yellow lines,
on your front drive for all he'd know –

but there was just a nagging shame, a covert wish
for tickets tucked behind the wiper-blades – same as before.

Eva

at fifteen months

The way your small head turns,
you could be networking
at a cocktail party or a waitress
trying not to catch my eye,
a barmaid serving someone else –
worse, a lone woman waiting
for the last tube. I want to tell you,
once, during a bomb scare,
I received an unexpected parcel
wrapped in plain brown paper,
which turned out to contain
a single orchid, whose stem
was immersed in a crystal
scent bottle, filled with water.

Eva

at seventeen months

You're baffled by the miracle
that stretches a glossy filament
from nostril to extended fingertip,
like the first finely spun dragline
of a spider's web. For a moment
you're Descartes, meditating
on the mind-body problem.
Could there be a hidden spinneret,
small as a pea at the brain's core,
another watery eye inside your head?
Is this the soul's elastic humour?
Then you gift me the thread,
my palm crossed with silver –
spiderlings joined by a silk hair,
ballooning over the Pacific,
so light we could land anywhere,
thousands of miles from the start.

Needlework

at twenty-three months

Just months in the weaving
now here's the wrap, the cover,
tangled as the purled shawl
in which her newborn sister lies.
The silver-tongued thread,
the gentle-hold-and-drop-stitch,
cross-stitch, unintended-bang-
the-feeding-baby stitch,
the sibling stitch up, the love
crush, the light-as-a-feather
needlepoint, the gros point,
saintly smile – that life so short,
the craft so quick to learn.

Canzone

after Petrarch No. 3

That Good Friday you nailed me.
I saw the sun shine out of your eyes
And was burnt before I knew it,
Before I had a chance to see
Just how love does its work,
Hits you when you least expect,
Strikes like a lightning fork
And leaves you wrecked,
Vulnerable as a frightened child
Crying his eyes out –
I'm shafted like a wild
Boar on a spit. How come
I stay hurt, and nothing penetrates
your bullet-proof vest?

Anniversary

Some things fatigue faster than others.
It took ten years for the handle
of this coal shovel to begin to flex,
fifty for my left knee to stop,
ten days for these reading glasses
to become unhinged. And us,
by rights rusty as old nails,
still unoxidised. Have I been white zinc
clinging to your iron all this time,
improbably galvanised at St Pancras
Town Hall with the Red Flag flying?
You in your Mary Quant and just two witnesses,
late because they thought we were joking,
causing a queue to build up outside.
Was it 1960s' inconsequential hip?
Remember the till on a trestle table:
'You may kiss the bride that'll be five pounds'
– our church bell, our starting call.

Arrhythmia

It was as if a pigeon had been trapped,
fallen from its chimney perch
half-starved behind the mantel –
wings flailing against the brick
setting an avalanche of twigs
and grit, gobbets of dry bread,
crumbling mortar, clots of soot,
feathers adrift, the frightened tremor
of its inner movement revealed
through the resonance of the wall –
a faint coo-coo, dying to be heard.

Unexpected Item in Nagging Area

A pair of fresh ginger cats,
some mixed organic hedge,
half-a-dozen free-range egotists,
a refuge for battered fish,
one lengthy vanilla podcast,
two ice-cold letters,
four large bunions,
a jar of artificial hearts,
three extra-virgin tarts,
a gang of violent beetroots,
skip bagging,
a box of crispy matadors,
a bucket of undetected leeks,
one tuberous yammer,
a platter of cooked meetings,
two ready-made seals,
a carton of ground black poodles,
one large waterfelon,
a medium green chilly morning,
a packet of frozen seas,
thank you for shopping
at **Lemon Zest**.

Dazzlement

a fuzzy feeling the hint of
some cool jazz in the air

it happens mostly in my bed
thinking about zed zed

strange really the words that turn me
on a bull's pizzle or

the creaking mizzen mast of an
old oak tea cutter or

the leather muzzle round the nose
of a wild rottweiler

sizzling Chinese beef dipped in black
bean sauce with egg fried rice

or getting sozzled on bottles
of fizzy french white wine

tell me about it you say what
poets need for a buzz

it's not the same what an s does
all that verbal razzamatazz

Glaze

They were in a dusty window on the High,
Dick Turpin and Tom King,
indigo blue topcoats crackled with age,
one on a black mount the other on a white,
as if the potter who'd fashioned them
really believed there was honour among thieves.

They could've been waiting for someone
to deliver a Dressage Rosette or both
subject to the same delusion – Napoleon,
in a cocked hat, after the Battle of Austerlitz.
Gentlemen Jacks in mustard cravats
but each with a flintlock casually held.

You'd as soon keep the Krays'
mug-shots on your mantelpiece,
or a figure of Ronnie Biggs,
with or without the cosh.
Call it bad taste sold them to me –
Staffordshire thugs with a patina of swash.

Spectacle Case

When pushed too far,
it fastens like the blade
of a Swiss Army knife,
the jaws of a ring-binder –
a judgment, a that's-itness,
a sprung trap, fisted as the clack
of a castanet. No going back,
what's inside's covered
by a carapace scalloped shut.
Pointless now pressing the point,

the subject's closed as
– 'anyhow'. Open and shut
till the clip wears down
and the lid's grip gives
like a beaten arm-wrestler.
There's pathos in the way
those glassy eyes still seek shelter
not knowing the mouth's unhinged,
the lock's lapsed and everything
'll end up hanging out.

Elbow Crutch

Its cuff grips your arm,
as if you were a blind woman
crossing the road.

Its telescopic leg
never leaves your side,
like a lover

intimate with your nakedness.
Its hand, clutched,
as if you were landing

during a period of turbulence.
And when you're down,
it's the ticket

for a secret lift,
and lets you in
to a world of casual kindness.

Knees

Everywhere a wasteland of clapped out muscle,
unhinged wheely-bins overflowing with trash;
if you scope the comings and goings,
you'll find a murky dive,
where inarticulate jerks and low-lifes
meet in an overcrowded space –
a steamy room with loose bodies
locked in unusual positions,
caught on camera, moving slowly,
if at all. A tenor sax bends *Mood Indigo*
through its horn and behind the bar
a notice tells you not to ask for credit
as a refusal often offends. There are beds
out the back and the floor's wet, where bits
of ragged tissue have been left around since
something went, after a night on the tiles.
Who knows which gang's running the protection
racket in those crooked joints, nothing like the bee's.

Rogue Hair

I
t's
alo
ne
in
my
eye
bro
w an
alb
ino
hair
that
slowly
but surely
incr
eases
in length
until
one
day I
notice
its jut
a proboscis
antenna or
narrow horn
emerging
from a
nest of
brown an
d grey lik
e some cu
ckoo's off
spring tha
t won't be
satisfied i
t wants
to grow a
nd grow a
single filam
ent of white
head and
shoulders
above the
rest like
a silver
birch in
a copse
seeking
the light
no matter
that I cut it
down over
and again
it comes
back to ha
unt the fron
t of my face
had I the gu
ts of a wom
an you're al
ways tellin
g me I woul
d pluck it out

Amputation Clinic

That gravel-crunch as you reverse
 Out of my life each morning
Wearing a thin integument of casual-smart
 Soft-sculpture I watched go on.
Soon you'll be at your desk swallowing
 Frustration, trying to break bad news
Gently offering yourself, the messenger
 To be over-killed before I see you back.

I don't know how you tell a man
 He'll never walk or recommend
A metal hook to someone for a hand
 That won't caress again –
Worse (by far I'd have to say) for them,
 Yet your going makes me think
I could be waiting there outside the door
 Ready to show my stump.

Chance Encounter with my Grandmother

The odds of meeting you on the Nevskiy Prospekt
must have been verging on a billion to one,
especially since you were born in Minsk,
Belarus, considerably further south than St Petersburg
more than a hundred and twenty years earlier.
Yet there you were – walking toward me
through the snow, surprisingly sure-footed
among a mass of bobbing hats and coats.

Your fur was out of fashion, as were your
flat-soled boots, and you were carrying
two shopping bags, one in each hand,
full of provisions. I saw you glance down
and tut as you crossed the Anichov Bridge,
where beer bottles and empty cans had been
chucked into the Fontanka, frozen into a carpet
of snow and ice and slush, littered like the bedroom

floor of a teenage boy. Opposite the Literary Café,
where Pushkin, having been dubbed, "Grand Master
of the Most Serene Order of Cuckolds",
waited for his fatal duel with Georges d'Anthès,
we ran right into one another. You seemed deeply
unimpressed and as I kissed your cheek, warned me
against poetry, not to get any meshúgga ideas,
or fritter away my time on a ganze megíllah.

Names

London, 1954

On Fridays just before sunset,
mother lit candles for the Sabbath.
We thanked the King of the Universe
for the fruit of the vine, the gift
of bread from the earth, the beauty
of the day coming in like a bride.
At sunrise we woke to a stillness,
washed and reminded ourselves
there was only one God –
begged that our lips be opened,
our mouths declare His praise.
Clad in our best for synagogue
we walked the three-quarter mile,
my father's trilby, my school-cap
raised in unison to ladies passing by.
A silk tallith draped over his shoulders
like the stole on a ball-gown,
Rabbi Rabinovitz unfurled the scrolls,
a silver finger pointing the way –
parchment teeming with tiny black fauna,
each one with a pop-star's quiff:
.DAL EHT OTNU DNAH YHT HTROF HCTERTS TON OD
.MIH OTNU MRAH YNA UOHT OD REHTIEN
After the service I ran home through
the playing fields of Gladstone Park,
passing ruffians calling – Jew, Jew-boy.

Cracow

So this is the old country –
where we blew in each year
with a tekiah godolah,
cast all our sins to the depths of the sea.

The Lady with an Ermine looking sideways
out of the Czartoryski Museum
at an exhibition of kitsch on the city wall.
Heaps of snow are peeing in the kerbside,

waiting to disappear.
The pigeons are doing their usual thing,
strutting and nodding in outsize charcoal uniforms.
In front of a shoe shop called *The Athlete's Foot*,

my umbrella's inverted by the wind.
Winkle-picker-chic women
are watching their stilettos in the tramlines
heading for the Jagiellonian University

and Pope John Paul is blessing us in bronze.
At the lobby of the Hotel Francuski, a porter asks
if I'd like to visit Auschwitz or the salt mine?

Footprints

You kept a record
of my first tooth,
first word, first steps.

Leaving the house now
after all those years,
my bootmarks are diamonds

in the mud outside
your door. Next winter
the sole's lattice will be pressed

in the memory of snow,
lasting only
as long as the thaw

and in time my track faint
as rain, nothing but a ripple
of displaced water.

Your Last Story

When I was young and couldn't sleep,
you told me about the Albert Hall
on Saint Cecilia's day; a vacant piano stool,
waiting page-turner. The fluttering hands
that entered through a skylight,
dropped like a gannet to open an arpeggio.

I'm at the bedside now and you're in pyjamas,
propped and heaving like a broken pump.
We've been here more than once,
the night scare, the fibrillation.
But this time it's different, oxygen
hissing from a cylinder and you

throttled by the tide's crescendo. The sea's
inked your lips indelibly blue, cold-fingered
your skin and widened the blacks of your eyes.
What story shall I tell? The undertow against
our clasped hands as you're tugged out
– followed by white gulls, white water.

Notes

THE REINCARNATION OF LEAVES, p.11
Bija niyama is the Buddhist principle of biological causality.

SWARM, p.23
For Terry Barry.

GEEST STAR, p.25
Banana boat, 1968.

MELTEMI, p.26
Is the Turkish name for a North-Westerly wind that blows across
the Aegean Sea.

THE LANGUAGE OF SMALL FISHING BOATS, p.27
Selimiye, Turkey.

BYNG, p.31
Admiral John Byng was executed on board HMS Monarch at noon
14 March 1757.

CONSERVATION STUDIO: HERMITAGE, p.34
For Lara Broecke.

YUCCA MOTH, p.35
San Christobal de Las Casas, Mexico.

COCKSURE, p.39
Cambridge, 1970. For Ivan Scrase.

RELICS, p.40
London, 1950.

CHIMAERA, p.42
Hampstead Heath, 1957.
For Jonathan Wilson.

FROM THE ANATOMY ROOM, p.43
Royal Free Hospital Medical School, 1962.

UNEXPECTED ITEM IN NAGGING AREA, p.53
DIY checkout in M&S food store, 2007.

DAZZLEMENT,p.54
For Matthew Francis.

KNEES, p.58
For Kate Wilson.

CHANCE ENCOUNTER WITH MY GRANDMOTHER, p.61
St Petersburg, 2004. In Yiddish 'meshúgga' means crazy, 'ganze
megíllah' means, in this context ironically, a long book with
aspirations to literary merit.

NAMES, p.62
London, 1954.

CRACOW, p.63
Tekiah godolah is a long note sounded on a ram's horn.

GREENWICH EXCHANGE BOOKS

POETRY

Adam's Thoughts in Winter *by Warren Hope*
Warren Hope's poems have appeared from time to time in a number of literary periodicals, pamphlets and anthologies on both sides of the Atlantic. They appeal to lovers of poetry everywhere. His poems are brief, clear, frequently lyrical, characterised by wit, but often distinguished by tenderness. The poems gathered in this first book-length collection counter the brutalising ethos of contemporary life, speaking of, and for, the virtues of modesty, honesty and gentleness in an individual, memorable way.
2000 • 46 pages • ISBN 978-1-871551-40-2

Baudelaire: Les Fleurs du Mal *Translated by F.W. Leakey*
Selected poems from *Les Fleurs du Mal* are translated with parallel French texts and are designed to be read with pleasure by readers who have no French as well as those who are practised in the French language.
F.W. Leakey was Professor of French in the University of London. As a scholar, critic and teacher he specialised in the work of Baudelaire for 50 years and published a number of books on the poet.
2001 • 152 pages • ISBN 978-1-871551-10-5

'The Last Blackbird' and other poems by Ralph Hodgson *edited and introduced by John Harding*
Ralph Hodgson (1871-1962) was a poet and illustrator whose most influential and enduring work appeared to great acclaim just prior to, and during, the First World War. His work is imbued with a spiritual passion for the beauty of creation and the mystery of existence. This new selection brings together, for the first time in 40 years, some of the most beautiful and powerful 'hymns to life' in the English language.
John Harding lives in London. He is a freelance writer and teacher and is Ralph Hodgson's biographer.
2004 • 70 pages • ISBN 978-871551-81-5

Lines from the Stone Age *by Sean Haldane*
Reviewing Sean Haldane's 1992 volume *Desire in Belfast*, Robert Nye wrote in *The Times* that "Haldane can be sure of his place among the

English poets." This place is not yet a conspicuous one, mainly because his early volumes appeared in Canada, and because he has earned his living by other means than literature. Despite this, his poems have always had their circle of readers. The 60 previously unpublished poems of *Lines from the Stone Age* – "lines of longing, terror, pride, lust and pain" – may widen this circle.

2000 • 52 pages • ISBN 978-1-871551-39-6

Lipstick *by Maggie Butt*
Lipstick is Maggie Butt's debut collection of poems and marks the entrance of a voice at once questioning and self-assured. She believes that poetry should be the tip of the stiletto which slips between the ribs directly into the heart. The poems of *Lipstick* are often deceptively simple, unafraid of focusing on such traditional themes as time, loss and love through a range of lenses and personae. Maggie Butt is capable of speaking in the voice of an 11th-century stonemason, a Himalayan villager, a 13-year-old anorexic. When writing of such everyday things as nylon sheets, jumble sales, X-rays or ginger beer, she brings to her subjects a dry humour and an acute insight. But beyond the intimate and domestic, her poems cover the world, from Mexico to Russia; they deal with war, with the resilience of women, and, most of all, with love.
Maggie Butt is head of Media and Communication at Middlesex University, London, where she has taught Creative Writing since 1990.

2007 • 72 pages • ISBN 978-1-871551-94-5

Martin Seymour-Smith – Collected Poems *edited by Peter Davies*
To the general public Martin Seymour-Smith (1928-1998) is known as a distinguished literary biographer, notably of Robert Graves, Rudyard Kipling and Thomas Hardy. To such figures as John Dover Wilson, William Empson, Stephen Spender and Anthony Burgess, he was regarded as one of the most independently-minded scholars of his generation, through his pioneering critical edition of Shakespeare's *Sonnets*, and his magisterial *Guide to Modern World Literature*.
To his fellow poets, Graves, James Reeves, C.H. Sisson and Robert Nye – he was first and foremost a poet. As this collection demonstrates, at the centre of the poems is a passionate engagement with Man, his sexuality and his personal relationships.

2006 • 182 pages • ISBN 978-1-871551-47-1

Shakespeare's Sonnets *by Martin Seymour-Smith*
Martin Seymour-Smith's outstanding achievement lies in the field of literary biography and criticism. In 1963 he produced his comprehensive edition, in the old spelling, of *Shakespeare's Sonnets* (here revised and corrected by himself and Peter Davies in 1998). With its landmark introduction and its brilliant critical commentary on each sonnet, it was praised by William Empson and John Dover Wilson. Stephen Spender said of him "I greatly admire Martin Seymour-Smith for the independence of his views and the great interest of his mind"; and both Robert Graves and Anthony Burgess described him as the leading critic of his time. His exegesis of the *Sonnets* remains unsurpassed.
2001 • 194 pages • ISBN 978-1-871551-38-9

The Rain and the Glass *by Robert Nye*
When Robert Nye's first poems were published, G.S. Fraser declared in the *Times Literary Supplement*: "Here is a proper poet, though it is hard to see how the larger literary public (greedy for flattery of their own concerns) could be brought to recognize that. But other proper poets – how many of them are left? – will recognise one of themselves."
Since then Nye has become known to a large public for his novels, especially *Falstaff* (1976), winner of the Hawthornden Prize and The Guardian Fiction Prize, and *The Late Mr Shakespeare* (1998). But his true vocation has always been poetry, and it is as a poet that he is best known to his fellow poets.
This book contains all the poems Nye has written since his *Collected Poems* of 1995, together with his own selection from that volume. An introduction, telling the story of his poetic beginnings, affirms Nye's unfashionable belief in inspiration, as well as defining that quality of unforced truth which distinguishes the best of his work: "I have spent my life trying to write poems, but the poems gathered here came mostly when I was not."
2005 • 132 pages • ISBN 978-1-871551-41-9

Wilderness *by Martin Seymour-Smith*
This is Martin Seymour-Smith's first publication of his poetry for more than twenty years. This collection of 36 poems is a fearless account of an inner life of love, frustration, guilt, laughter and the celebration of others. He is best known to the general public as the author of the controversial and bestselling *Hardy* (1994).
1994 • 52 pages • ISBN 978-1-871551-08-2